This book is dedicated to

my mom

for gathering all of the supplies
and for taking me on all kinds of adventures
to do the pictures.
I couldn't have done it without her!

Other titles by Heléna Macalino

Picture Books

The Reflection

AUTHOR:
HELENA MACALINO

ILLUSTRATOR:
JUSTYNA PAWLUCZUK

Wish Fish Early Readers

The Book of Slime

by Helena Macauna

33 Recipes for Stretchy, Twisty, Squishy Fun!

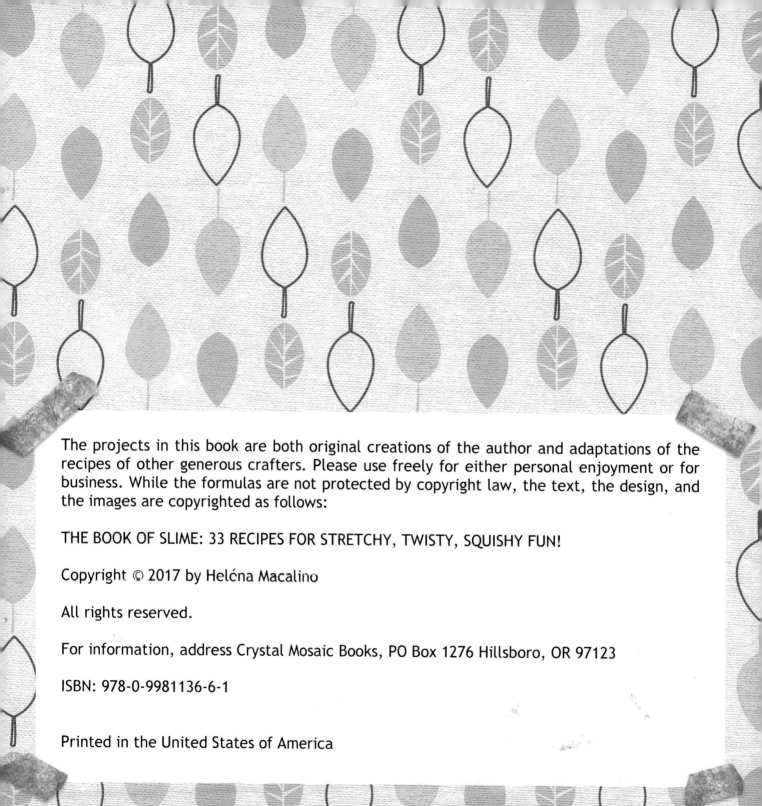

THE BOOK OF SLIME: 33 RECIPES FOR STRETCHY, TWISTY, SQUISHY FUN!

Copyright © 2017 by Heléna Macalino

For information, address Crystal Mosaic Books, PO Box 1276 Hillsboro, OR 97123

ISBN: 978-0-9981136-6-1

Printed in the United States of America

Safety/Legal Note:
I know these sorts of notices make things sound scary, but as we all know, they have become necessary. So, here it goes: "The author does not accept responsibility for effects arising from following these recipes or from the use of these products. These products are not intended for children under the age of 3."

Please use caution using slime around carpet, cloth, or hair.

There, it's over. Now let's go have fun!

Table of Contents

Author's Note

Hello fellow slime lover!

I bet you are wondering how a fiction writer ended up publishing a book of slime recipes. Well, I've always been a slime and putty collector. I would save up the money from my books to buy cans of Aaron's Thinking Putty™. Expensive!

I can't remember how I stumbled across my first slime recipe, but I do remember thinking, "I can make this myself?!" I was hooked!

My first batch was a simple concoction of glitter glue and Sta-Flo. (We had the Sta-Flo in an old science kit. The hardest part was talking my dad into buying the bottle of glitter glue!) Boy, was he nervous about me getting it stuck to everything! But pretty soon my friend Olivia and I were slime-making masters!

I hope this book brings tons of slime-making fun to crafters outside the YouTube world! Slime is unlike any other fidget you've ever tried. Each slime has a different texture and stretchiness and when you make it yourself, you can make it whatever color or level of stickiness you want! You can shape it and stretch it into any form your imagination can picture. Then watch it melt back down for the next round of fun!

Let the good times begin!

Heléna

The Kitchen Chemist

PS - Don't forget to check out the Troubleshooting page in the back of the book, if you run into any trouble with your slime!

Glue
Slimes

OG Slime

Ingredients

1 bottle Elmer's School Glue®

Purex Sta-Flo Liquid Starch®

Equipment

Mixing bowl
Mixing utensil

Directions

1) Pour the glue into a bowl.

2) Add Sta-Flo little by little until your slime starts to come together.

3) Knead your slime until you have your preferred amount of stickiness.

4) Add more Sta-Flo if your slime is still too sticky.

Notes from the Kitchen Chemist

If you are just making OG (Original) Slime for fun and not as a base for another slime recipe, try folding in a few drops of food coloring!

Liquid Glass Slime

Ingredients

1 bottle Elmer's Washable Clear School Glue®

3 ½ Tbsp Contact solution

2 Tbsp Water

1 ¼ cup Warm water

2 tsp Baking soda

Equipment

Mixing bowl

Mixing utensil

Air-tight storage container

Directions

1) Pour clear glue into the bowl.

2) Add contact solution and 2 Tbsp water. Mix gently.

3) In separate bowl, mix 1 ¼ cup warm water and baking soda.

4) Pour glue mixture into the baking soda water. Do not mix.

5) Strain excess baking soda water out.

6) If remaining slime is too sticky, add more contact solution.

7) Put the slime into an air-tight container for 4-5 days and let the air bubbles rise out until the slime is clear.

Notes from the Kitchen Chemist

You can stretch this slime out into a window and it's like it's not even there, it's so clear. If you find that the air bubbles come back, just put it back in the container overnight and they should go away!

Glitz & Glam Glitter Slime

Ingredients

1 bottle Elmer's Classic Glitter Glue® (favorite color)

Purex Sta-Flo Liquid Starch®

Equipment

Mixing bowl
Mixing utensil

Directions

1) Pour the glitter glue into a bowl.

2) Add Sta-Flo little by little until your slime starts to come together.

3) Knead your slime until you have your preferred amount of stickiness.

4) Add more Sta-Flo if your slime is still too sticky.

Notes from the Kitchen Chemist

This is my favorite slime! It has such a cool texture and it has a neat pearliness. Plus, there are so many varieties of glitter glue!

Fluffy Slime

Ingredients

1 bottle Elmer's School Glue®

Purex Sta-Flo Liquid Starch®

Shaving foam (favorite scent)

Optional food coloring

Equipment

Mixing bowl

Mixing utensil

Directions

1) Pour the glue into a bowl.

2) Add shaving foam a handful at a time until you achieve your desired fluffiness.

3) Add Sta-Flo little by little until your slime starts to come together.

4) Knead your slime until you have your preferred amount of stickiness.

5) Fold in a few drops of food coloring if you want it.

Notes from the Kitchen Chemist

Keep in mind, the more shaving foam you add, the fluffier and bigger batch you will get! (Just not so much that it loses its slimey-ness.)

24k Pearl Gold Slime

Ingredients

3 grams Solar Gold Jacquard Pearl Ex Powdered Pigment

1 bottle Elmer's Washable Clear School Glue®

Purex Sta-Flo Liquid Starch®

Equipment

Mixing bowl
Mixing utensil

Directions

1) Pour the bottle of clear glue into a bowl.

2) Add gold Pearl Ex Powder Pigment and stir to combine.

3) Add small amounts of Sta-Flo at a time until your slime forms!

Notes from the Kitchen Chemist

The first time I tried this recipe, I used the contact lens solution and baking soda method, but the next day when I took it out of the container to play with it, I found it wouldn't stick to itself. I definitely recommend the Sta-Flo method.

Fluffy Pearl Glitter Slime

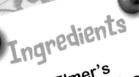

Ingredients

1 bottle Elmer's Classic Glitter Glue® (favorite color)

Shaving foam (favorite scent)

Purex Sta-Flo Liquid Starch®

Equipment

Mixing bowl
Mixing utensil

Directions

1) Pour the bottle of glitter glue into a bowl.

2) Add shaving foam a handful at a time until you achieve your desired fluffiness.

3) Add small amounts of Sta-Flo at a time until your slime forms!

Notes from the Kitchen Chemist

This slime has a natural pearliness to it that shines through when you stretch it!

Butter Slime

Ingredients

1 batch of "OG" Slime

4 oz package Yellow Crayola Model Magic Clay®

Equipment

Mixing bowl
Mixing utensil

Directions

1) Make one batch of "OG Slime" from page 3.

2) Add Model Magic Clay. Knead until fully combined.

Notes from the Kitchen Chemist

This slime has the most amaaaaazing texture and it spreads just like butter

Honey Slime

Ingredients

1 bottle Elmer's Washable Clear School Glue®

1/4 drop of red food coloring (use a toothpick as a mini dropper)

2 drops of yellow food coloring

Purex Sta-Flo Liquid Starch®

Equipment

Mixing bowl

Mixing utensil

Mason jar

Toothpick

Directions

1) Pour the bottle of clear glue into a bowl.

2) Add food coloring and mix well.

3) Add small amounts of Sta-Flo at a time until your slime forms!

Notes from the Kitchen Chemist

You can use a mason jar to make your honey slime look real honey and use a spoon to drizzle it—just like in the picture!

Silver Slime

Ingredients

1 bottle Elmer's Washable Clear School Glue®

1 container Silver Sky L'Oreal Infallible Eye Shadow®

Purex Sta-Flo Liquid Starch®

Optional lotion (favorite scent)

Equipment

Mixing bowl
Mixing utensil

Directions

1) Pour the bottle of clear glue into a bowl.

2) Add eye shadow and mix well.

3) Add small amounts of Sta-Flo at a time until your slime forms!

4) Add lotion to make this slime more stretchy and softer, if you like.

Notes from the Kitchen Chemist

This slime is wonderfully soft and stretchy. I found that if I used the baking soda and contact lens solution method for this slime, the next day it ripped very easily and wouldn't stretch. (If that's the kind of slime you are after, go ahead and try it!)

Glue-Free Slimes

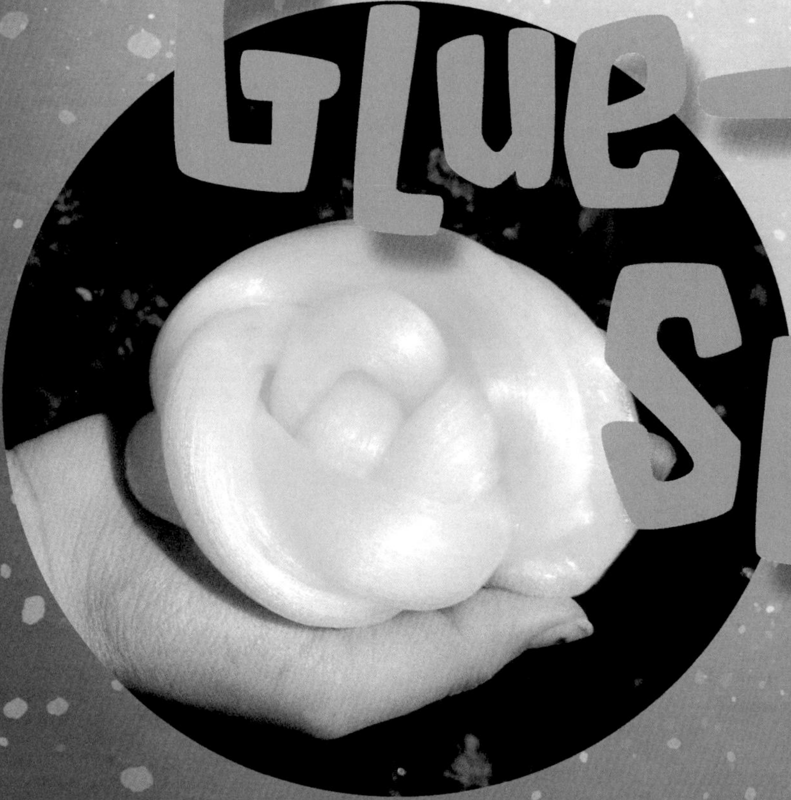

Lily Pad Stretchy Slime

Ingredients

4 oz package Green Crayola Model Magic Clay®

Shaving foam (favorite scent)

Equipment

Mixing bowl

Directions

1) Put the Model Magic Clay in a bowl.

2) Knead handfuls of shaving cream into the clay until it is soft and stretchy.

Notes from the Kitchen Chemist

This recipe turns out more dough-like than slime-like, but it is still very stretchy and has a cool matte finish to it!

Jelly Swamp Slime

Ingredients

2-in-1 Watermelon Suave Kids shampoo and conditioner

Equipment

Plate

Directions

1) Squeeze the amount of 2-in-1 you want to turn into slime onto the plate.

2) Leave uncovered overnight.

3) If it is still sticky the next morning, leave alone for another day.

4) Transfer to an airtight container for storage.

Notes from the Kitchen Chemist

Who knew you could leave shampoo on the table and it would be slime the next morning? How fun!

Spa Slime

Ingredients

Peel-off face mask containing polyvinyl alcohol

Contact lens solution containing boric acid

Baking soda

Equipment

Mixing bowl
Mixing utensil

Directions

1) Squeeze your bottle of peel-off face mask into a bowl

2) Sprinkle a small amount of baking soda over the mask gel and mix it in.

3) Add small amounts of contact lens solutions until slime forms.

Notes from the Kitchen Chemist

This slime smells amazing. Just like a day at the spa!

Blu-Tack Slime

Ingredients

75g Blu-Tack
Reusable Adhesive®

Liquid hand soap

Optional lotion
(favorite scent)

Equipment

Mixing bowl

Directions

1) Knead Blu-Tack until it softens a bit.

2) Pump two squirts of hand soap into the bowl.

3) Dip the ball of Blu-Tack into the soap and knead, repeat until the ball softens. (This will take a while!)

4) Add a small portion of lotion to soften your slime, if desired.

Notes from the Kitchen Chemist

This slime is like playing with melted marshmallow amazingness! When you stretch it, it feels rubber, but it is still super stretchy. Don't add too much soap or the slime will become extremely sticky and leave goo all over your hands!

Novelty Slimes

Gallium Slime

Ingredients

¼ batch of Liquid Glass Slime

1g Silver Mirror Nail Powder

Equipment

Mixing bowl

Mixing utensil

Directions

1) Make one batch of Liquid Glass Slime from page 5.

2) Place a quarter of the Liquid Glass Slime in a bowl.

3) Add the Silver Mirror Nail Powder and mix well.

Notes from the Kitchen Chemist

Gallium is a nontoxic metal which when warmed in water becomes a liquid metal that you can touch—and it kinda reminds me of slime. So why not make a slime just like it—a melted mirror!

Pick Up Putty

Ingredients

Borax

Water

1 bottle Elmer's School Glue®

Optional food coloring

Equipment

Tall Pitcher

Skewer

Directions

1) Pour 4 cups of hot water in the pitcher.

2) Add 1 Tbsp borax to the water and mix until dissolved.

3) Stir the solution with the skewer to get it whirling really well.

4) Squeeze the white glue through the nozzle into the pitcher.

5) Stir the glue with the skewer. It should start to gather on the skewer.

6) Pull the putty out of the water and begin kneading it.

7) If it remains too sticky, give it another swirl in the borax water.

Notes from the Kitchen Chemist

This putty slime is bouncy! It can also lift the print from newspapers—therefore the name! Yes, this recipe contains borax—in a safe dilution. Do not handle borax powder directly with your hands, eat, or drink it. Wash your hands when you are done mixing the putty.

Iceberg Slime

Ingredients

2 bottles Elmer's School Glue®

1 can shaving cream (favorite scent)

Blue food coloring

Purex Sta-Flo Liquid Starch®

Equipment

Large Mixing bowl
Large Mixing utensil

Directions

1) Pour 2 bottles of white glue into a LARGE bowl.

2) Spray an entire can of shaving cream into the bowl.

3) Add several drops of food coloring while mixing until you get your preferred "ocean" color.

4) Add small amounts of Sta-Flo at a time until your slime forms!

5) Let the Iceberg Slime sit out uncovered for 2-3 days until "ice" forms on the surface. Then reach in and crack it up!

Notes from the Kitchen Chemist

You can let this slime re-harden as many times as you want! Each time you'll have a new layer of "ice" to crack.

Fruit Salad Slime

Ingredients

1 batch of Liquid Glass Slime

One pouch of assorted fruit slices nail art

Equipment

Mixing bowl

Directions

1) Make one batch of Liquid Glass Slime from page 5.

2) Add your desired amount of fruit slices

Notes from the Kitchen Chemist

Fruit Salad Slime is fun to drizzle and watch the little fruits fall. You can also stretch it out, make a window, and see the fruits in the super clear slime.

Floam

Ingredients

½ bottle of Elmer's School Glue®

Purex Sta-Flo Liquid Starch®

1 pouch colored micro Styrofoam balls

Equipment

Mixing bowl
Mixing utensil

Directions

1) Pour the glue into a bowl.

2) Add Sta-Flo little by little until your slime starts to come together.

3) Knead your slime until you have a sticky slime.

4) Add Styrofoam balls and knead until all of the balls have been mixed in.

Notes from the Kitchen Chemist

When you stretch out floam it makes a cool spider web of slime and floam balls! This recipe can be a little tricky. You have to get just the right amount of stickiness to make it work, so be sure to get a backup bag of Styrofoam to practice with.

Cake Batter Slime

Ingredients

1 cup Elmer's School Glue®

1 cup Shaving foam (favorite scent)

½ cup Foaming hand soap

Yellow food coloring

Vanilla extract

Purex Sta-Flo Liquid Starch®

1 pouch rainbow micro Styrofoam balls

Equipment

Mixing bowl

Mixing utensil

Directions

1) Pour white glue into the bowl.

2) Add shaving cream and foaming hand soap. Mix well.

3) Add yellow food coloring a drop at a time until you get a cake batter color

4) Add vanilla until you like the scent.

5) Add small amounts of Sta-Flo at a time until your slime forms!

6) Sprinkle with a small amount of Styrofoam balls. Mix

Notes from the Kitchen Chemist

The awesome thing about this slime is that it smell, looks, and feels like cake batter, but you can play with it all you want!

Pebble Slime

Ingredients

1 batch of "OG" Slime

Polly Pellets (weighted stuffing beads)

Optional food coloring

Equipment

Mixing bowl

Mixing utensil

Directions

1) Make one batch of "OG Slime" from page 3; making sure to leave it a little sticky, so it will hold the beads.

2) Add Polly Pellets and mix in.

3) Fold in a few drops of food coloring if you want.

Notes from the Kitchen Chemist

Don't add too many beads or when you play with your slime, they will fall out and get everywhere!

Crunchy Slime

Ingredients

1 batch of Liquid Glass Slime

Clear plastic vase-filler pellets

Equipment

Mixing bowl

Mixing utensil

Directions

1) Make one batch of Liquid Glass Slime from page 5. (No need to wait for the air bubbles to rise, if you don't want to.)

2) Add the pellets a handful at a time until it is crunchy, but not so many that the pellets fall out every time you knead it.

Notes from the Kitchen Chemist

Crunching this slime in your hands is like playing with icy snow—without the freezing cold! To get it out of the container, tap the container upside down and the slime will fall out in one piece.

Candle Slime

Ingredients

10 oz Soy candle

10 oz Elmer's School Glue®

Purex Sta-Flo Liquid Starch®

Optional lotion (favorite scent)

Optional food coloring (if candle isn't colored)

Equipment

Mixing bowl

Mixing utensil

Double Boiler

Microwave

Whisk

Directions

1) Melt candle in a double boiler with the help of an adult until you can remove the metal wicks.

2) Turn candle upside down and remove from container. Pull out wicks, including metal bases.

3) Melt wax in 15 second increments in the microwave, stirring between heating until all wax is melt. Do not overheat wax.

4) SLOWLY add glue, while whisking to avoid creating chunks of wax.

5) If your candle is white, you can fold in a few drops of food coloring now.

5) Add small amounts of Sta-Flo at a time until your slime forms!

6) If your slime comes out too stiff, add lotion until it softens.

Notes from the Kitchen Chemist

Adding a candle gives slime such a nice cake batter feel and makes it fluffy and lovely!

Peach Smoothie Slime

Ingredients

1 batch of Liquid Glass Slime

2 drops Yellow food coloring

1 drop Red food coloring

Peach-scented lotion

Equipment

Mixing bowl

Mixing utensil

Directions

1) Make one batch of Liquid Glass Slime from page 5.

2) Add food coloring.

3) Add peach-scented lotion. Not too much or it will ruin the color of your slime!

Notes from the Kitchen Chemist

Peach slime has a unique milky consistency, but it still stays together. It smells magical and as an added bonus, as you play with it, it moisturizes your hands!

Ingredients

2 bottles Elmer's School Glue®

2 cups Shaving foam

2 fl oz Shimmer metallic-finish black acrylic paint

Fine red glitter

Purex Sta-Flo Liquid Starch®

Safari Good Luck Mini Animals

Optional: Foaming hand soap (favorite scent) & Pearl mica for extra shimmer

Black Hole Slime

Equipment

Mixing bowl

Mixing utensil

Directions

1) Pour white glue (8 oz) into the bowl.

2) Add shaving cream a handful at a time until you achieve your desired fluffiness.

3) Add paint. Mix well.

4) Add enough glitter to make a slight red shimmer in the black. (I used the whole bottle.)

5) Optional: Add scented foaming soap, if you feel the paint is stinking up your slime!

6) Optional: Add pearl mica for extra glow.

7) Add small amounts of Sta-Flo at a time until your slime forms!

8) Hide the mini toys in the Black Hole!

Notes from the Kitchen Chemist

It's a slime; it's a fidget; it's a whole new game! Each pull and stretch reveals a new animal. It's fun to pop them out and see which one you got!

Rice Crispy Slime

Ingredients

1 batch "OG" Slime

1 pouch yellow micro Styrofoam balls

Equipment

Mixing bowl
Mixing utensil

Directions

1) Make one batch of "OG Slime" from page 3.

2) Add pouch of yellow micro Styrofoam balls.

Notes from the Kitchen Chemist

Rice Crispy slime makes popping sounds just like the cereal when you play with it! I discovered this recipe the first time I tried making floam.

Magnetic Slime

Ingredients

1 batch of "OG" Slime

1 cup Synthetic black iron oxide

Optional lotion (favorite scent)

Equipment

Mixing bowl

Mixing utensil

Drop cloth to protect work surface

Directions

1) Make one batch of OG Slime from page 3.

2) CAREFULLY, add iron oxide, gently mix. (Iron oxide is very messy!)

3) If your slime comes out too stiff, add lotion until it softens.

Notes from the Kitchen Chemist

When you hold a super-strong magnet over the slime, a piece of the slime climbs toward the magnet all on its own. It's amazing!

Color-Changing Slime

Ingredients

2 batchs of Liquid Glass Slime

5 grams Temperature activated thermochromic bi-color powder pigment

Equipment

Mixing bowl

Mixing utensil

Directions

1) Make one batch of Liquid Glass Slime from page 5.

2) Add pigment and mix well.

Notes from the Kitchen Chemist

When you touch the slime, it changes color right before your eyes. After you've played with it for a while, it all becomes the new color. Then leave it alone, or put it in the refrigerator and it's ready to go again!

Glow-in-the-Dark Slime

Ingredients

¼ batch of Liquid Glass Slime

12 g Glow-in-the-dark pigment powder

Equipment

Mixing bowl
Mixing utensil

Directions

1) Make one batch of Liquid Glass Slime from page 5.

2) Add pigment powder to ¼ of the batch and mix well.

Notes from the Kitchen Chemist

When you aren't using the slime, put it in a clear container under a light so it can charge up! Then, when you are ready to play, go into dark room and it's so magical. It's like a glowing ball of light!

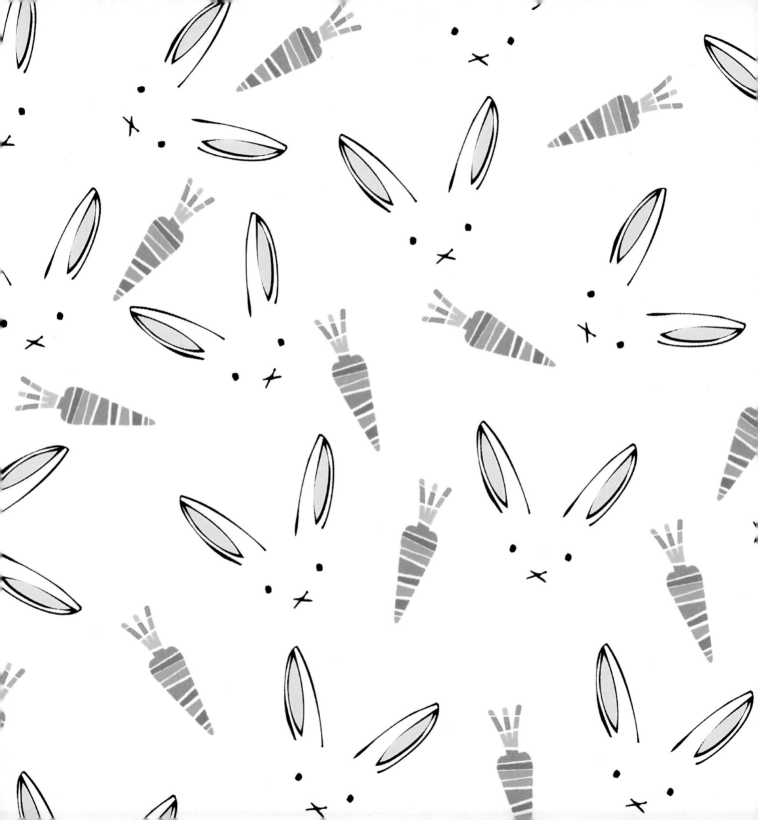

Edible Slimes

Gummy Bear Slime

Ingredients

2 large bags of gummy bears

½ cup Cornstarch

½ cup Powdered Sugar

Equipment

Two small mixing bowls

Mixing utensil

Directions

1) Separate gummy bears into two piles: red + orange, green + yellow.

2) Mix cornstarch and powdered sugar in a bowl. Set aside.

3) Place one pile of bears in a microwave safe bowl.

4) Microwave the bears in 10 second increments until they are completely melted. Use extreme caution: the melted bears can burn your skin.

5) Add the powder to your melted bears a spoonful at a time and mix.

6) When your mixture is thick and cool enough, continue to add powder a bit at a time but use your hands (coated in powder) to knead it until your slime comes together.

7) In the end, your slime will be stretchy and a little doughy, but still a little sticky.

Notes from the Kitchen Chemist

How cool is this?! It's stretchy, soft, and sweet-smelling. And you can eat it! In fact, if you don't eat it, it will get hard and even start to mold eventually. If your slime turns out too stiff, you've added too much powder. Give the recipe another try with your other pile of bears!

Orange Slime

Ingredients

1 cup Water

1 Tbsp Metamucil™

1 Tbsp Tang™ orange powdered drink mix

Equipment

Mixing bowl

Mixing utensil

Directions

1) Pour the water into a microwave safe bowl. Add Metamucil and Tang and mix well.

2) Set the microwave for five minutes. Every time the mixture starts to bubble up, open the microwave and wait for it to settle. Then continue microwaving.

3) Wait for it to cool before playing.

Notes from the Kitchen Chemist

This is a jello-y slime. It doesn't stretch very well, but it is very jiggly! Yes, it is edible, but careful not to overeat it. Metamucil makes you poop! Again, like all other edible slime, if kept unrefrigerated, it will start to mold.

Starburst™ Slime

Ingredients

1 large bag of Starburst

1 cup Powdered Sugar

Equipment

Two small mixing bowls

Mixing utensil

Directions

1) Separate Starburst into two piles: red + orange, green + yellow.

2) Place powdered sugar in a bowl. Set aside.

3) Place one pile of unwrapped Starburst in a microwave safe bowl.

4) Microwave the candy in 10 second increments until they are completely melted. Use extreme caution: the melted candy can burn your skin.

5) Add the sugar to your melted candy a spoonful at a time and mix.

6) When your mixture is thick and cool enough, continue to add sugar a bit at a time, but use your hands (coated in sugar) to knead it just until your slime is no longer sticky. (If you add too much, it will become a hard dough.)

Notes from the Kitchen Chemist

This is the slime for Starburst lovers! Share it with your friends while it is still warm or it will turn rock hard when it tries to return to its original form!

Hot Chocolate Slime

Ingredients

6 large Marshmallows

1 TBSP Coconut oil

4 rectangles of a Hershey's™ chocolate bar

½ cup of powdered sugar

Equipment

Two small mixing bowls

Mixing utensil

Directions

1) Place marshmallows in a microwave-safe bowl. Melt for 5 seconds.

2) Add coconut oil and melt for another 5 seconds.

3) Add chocolate and microwave until all ingredients are melted.

4) Mix all ingredients. Slowly add powdered sugar, spoonful by spoonful, until slime forms.

Notes from the Kitchen Chemist

This is the yummiest slime ever! It tastes just like chewy chocolate coconut fudge. This recipe is more doughy than slimey, but the taste is totally worth it! Again, this slime doesn't keep, so eat up!

Confetti Icing Slime

Ingredients

1 container Pillsbury Funfetti™ Icing

Powdered sugar

Equipment

Mixing bowl

Mixing utensil

Directions

1) Scoop icing into bowl.

2) Add powdered sugar ¼ cup at a time until you reach your desired consistency.

3) Add sprinkles!

Notes from the Kitchen Chemist

So simple and so pretty. Again, this slime doesn't keep, so eat up!

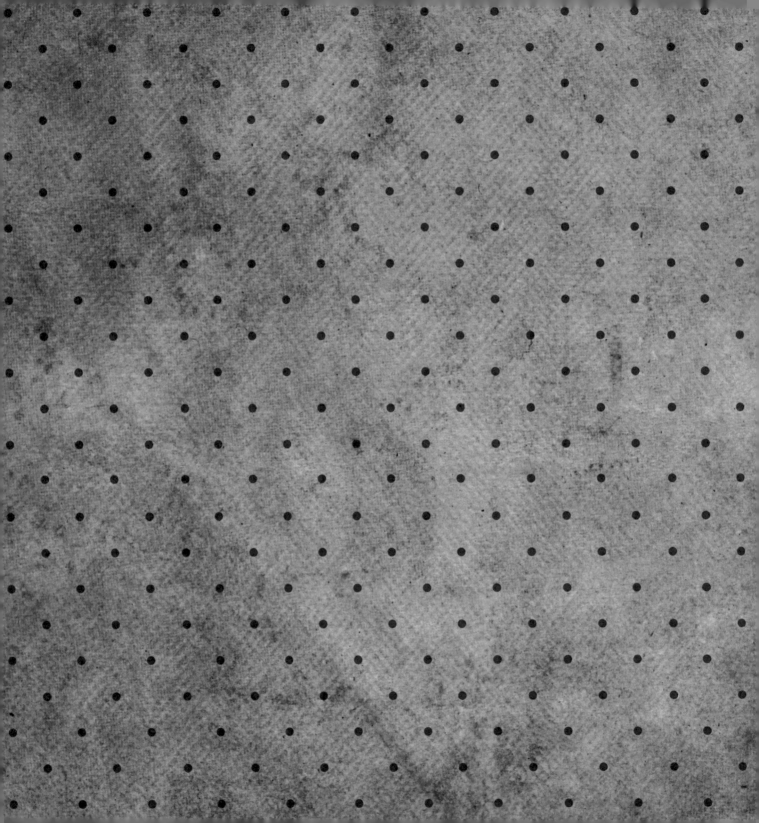

Other titles by Heléna Macalino

Picture Books

The Reflection

AUTHOR:
HELÉNA MACALINO

ILLUSTRATOR:
JUSTYNA PAWLUCZUK

Wish Fish Early Readers

The Mouse Bird
The Wish Fish Early Reader Series

Book 1

By Heléna Macalino
Illustrated by Milena Radeva

The Chipmunk King
The Wish Fish Early Reader Series

Book 2

By Heléna Macalino
Illustrated by Milena Radeva

The Winter Magpie
The Wish Fish Early Reader Series

Book 3

By Heléna Macalino
Illustrated by Milena Radeva

Join Helena's Reader Group

at www.fffacalino.com

and get free books and recipes!

Troubleshooting Your Slime

If your slime is too sticky...
Keep kneading! Add a little bit of Sta-Flo at a time until your slime stays together better.

If your slime is too stringy and slimey...
It probably has too much Sta-Flo or other activator. Add a little bit of glue at a time until the extra activator is absorbed.

If your slime is too stiff or tears too easily...
Add lotion to it a few pumps at a time until the slime becomes more flexible.

When you are done playing with your slime...
Store it in an airtight container away from the sun. Hot slime can turn into goo and even rot after a while. Slime exposed to the air will dry out and eventually lose its stretchiness.

Be prepared to learn...
When you are trying a new slime recipe, it may take you a few tries to get the recipe just the way you want it. That's how kitchen chemists work—we experiment!

About the Author

Heléna Macalino
loves to explore her dreams. She wanders along lovely garden paths with magical gates, finds her way into enchanted forests with animals who hide huge wishes in their hearts. And as a member of a family of writers, she records these adventures to share with fellow wanderers. Heléna wrote her first book when she was in 2nd grade, THE REFLECTION, an Alice in Wonderland style picture book about a little girl who falls through the reflection of a puddle. Now a 5th grader, Heléna is the proud author of 5 books with yet more coming soon.

Want to follow Heléna in her wanderings? When she's not cuddling with her bunny or concocting her latest slime creation, she can be found on her family's website www.macalino.com.

Subscribe to her **Reader Group** on the website and receive free books and recipes. You'll also be the very first to learn when she releases a new book!

Made in the USA
Middletown, DE
27 July 2018